MONKEY BUSINESS

Fun with Idioms

Laura Hambleton & Sedat Turhan
Illustrated by **Hervé Tullet**

Milet Publishing, LLC
333 North Michigan Avenue
Suite 530
Chicago, IL 60601
info@milet.com
www.milet.com

Monkey Business: Fun with Idioms
Text by Laura Hambleton and Sedat Turhan
Illustrations by Hervé Tullet

First published by Milet Publishing, LLC in 2006

ISBN-13: 978 1 84059 499 7
ISBN-10: 1 84059 499 3

Printed and bound in China

Please see our website **www.milet.com**
for other Milet Wordwise titles.

MILET
WORDWISE

MONKEY BUSINESS

Fun with Idioms

Laura Hambleton & Sedat Turhan

Illustrated by Hervé Tullet

PUT YOUR BEST FOOT FORWARD.

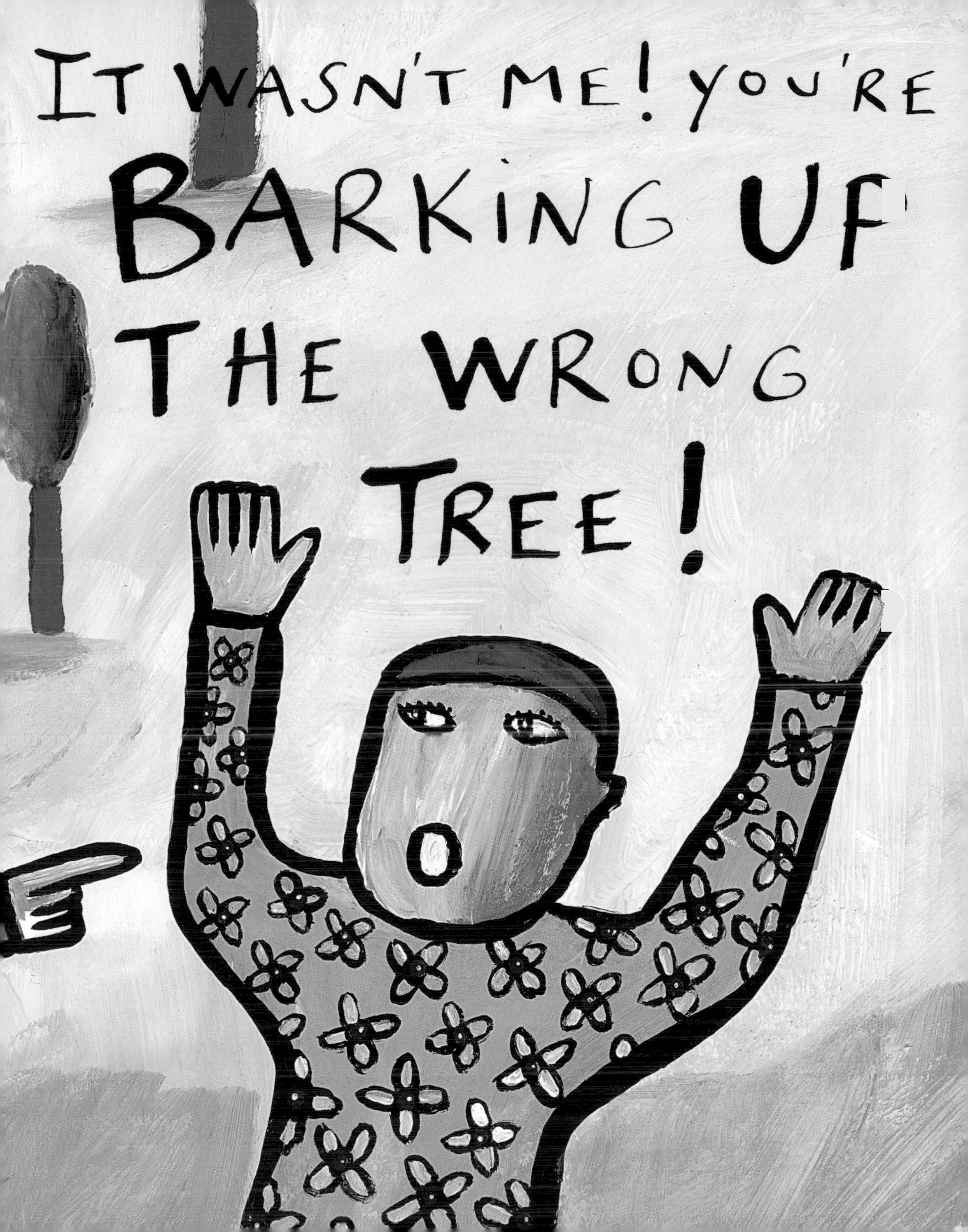
IT WASN'T ME! YOU'RE
BARKING UP
THE WRONG
TREE!

Too much TV makes you a couch potato.

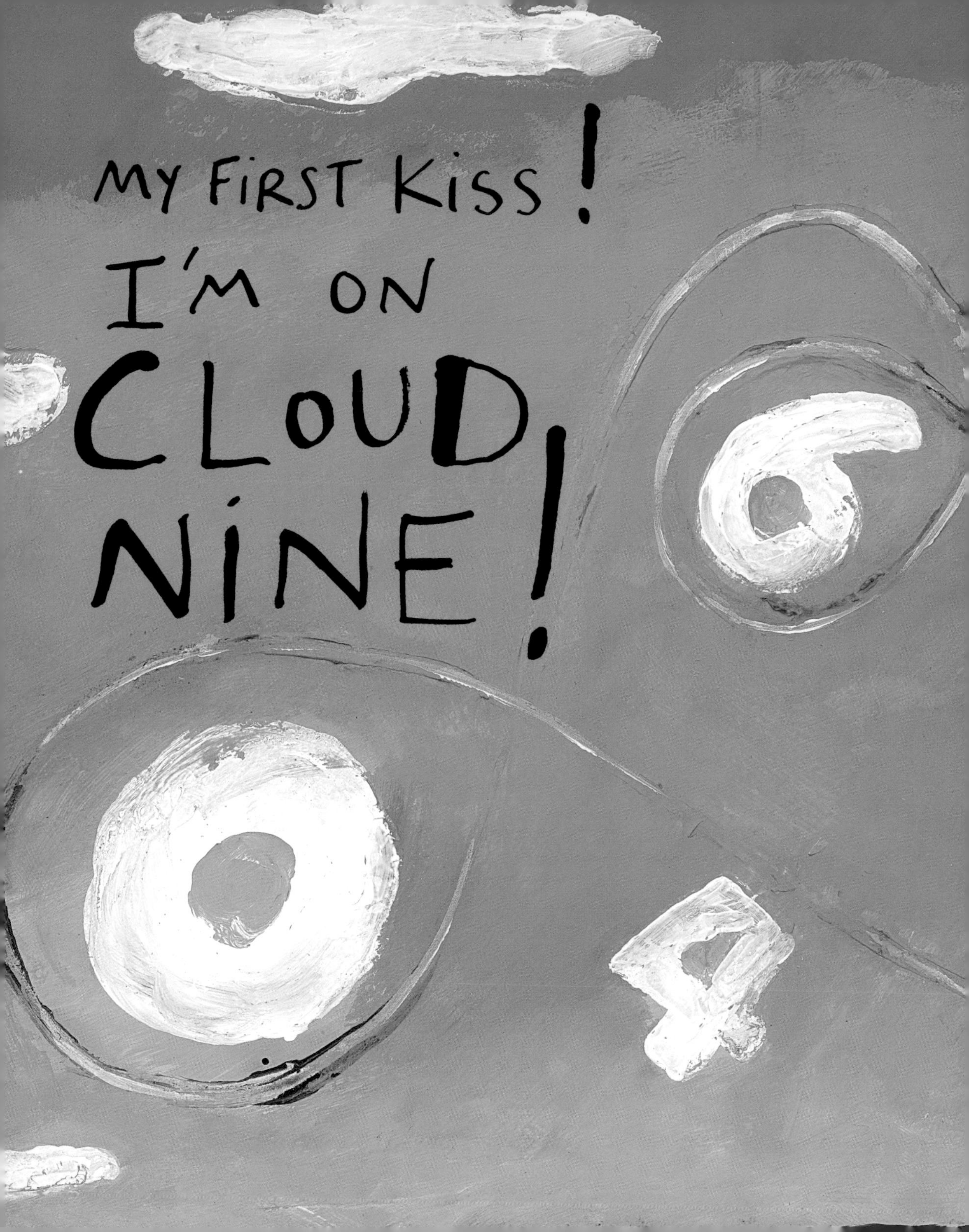
MY FIRST KISS!
I'M ON
CLOUD
NINE!

Idioms

An idiom is an expression that doesn't mean what you might expect from the meaning of the individual words.

1 When you **put your best foot forward**, you try to do your very best.

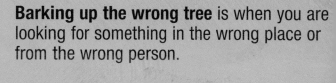

2 **Barking up the wrong tree** is when you are looking for something in the wrong place or from the wrong person.

3 **I'll give you a hand** means I will help you.

4 When I am **under the weather**, I am feeling a little ill.

5 When I am upset or angry about something, I am **bent out of shape**.

6 When you don't have a plan and decide what to do as you go along, you **play it by ear**.

7 A **couch potato** is someone who spends too much time sitting around and watching TV.

8 When you **read my mind**, you knew what I was thinking.

9 If I am sad about something, I am **down in the dumps**.

10 If I am **on cloud nine**, I am very happy.

11 **Monkey business** is silly or mischievous behaviour.

Other titles in the **Milet Wordwise** series

Telling Tails: Fun with Homonyms
Strawberry Bullfrog: Fun with Compound Words
Jump, Jog, Leapfrog: Fun with Action Words

Other Milet books by the creators of
Monkey Business: Fun with Idioms

Hervé Tullet

Alphabet Poem
Night & Day
Pink Lemon
Yellow & Round
Blue & Square

Laura Hambleton

English with Abby and Zak
Chameleon Races
Chameleon Swims
Welcome to Lizard Lounge
How Bees Be
I'm Afraid too!

Sedat Turhan

Milet Flashwords
Milet Mini Picture Dictionary
Milet Picture Dictionary

www.milet.com

3938